insight text guide

William Douglas

Great Short Works

Edgar Allan Poe

insight®

▸innovative ▸engaging ▸evolving

First published in 2007, reprinted 2010, 2012, 2016, 2022.

Insight Publications Pty Ltd
3/350 Charman Road
Cheltenham VIC 3192
Australia
Tel: +61 3 8571 4950
Fax: +61 3 8571 0257
Email: books@insightpublications.com.au

www.insightpublications.com.au

National Library of Australia Cataloguing-in-Publication entry:
Douglas, William (William Neville).
Edgar Allan Poe's Great short works.
For secondary school students.
ISBN 9781921088704 (pbk.).
1. Poe, Edgar Allan, 1809-1849. Great short works of Edgar Allan Poe. I. Title.
818.309

Cover design by Gisela Beer, based on a concept by The Modern Art Production Group

Printed in Australia by Ligare Book Printers

contents

CHARACTER TABLE

Story	Story type	Central character	Major relationship	Nature of major relationship	Minor relationships
'Berenice'	Gothic horror	Egæus	Berenice	E & B are cousins; become engaged	—
'The Fall of the House of Usher'	Gothic horror	narrator (unnamed)	Roderick Usher	Narrator is visiting R, a childhood friend	Madeline Usher (R's sister)
'William Wilson'	Gothic horror	William Wilson	William Wilson	WW's double represents his conscience	—
'The Murders in the Rue Morgue'	Detective	C. Auguste Dupin	narrator (unnamed)	Narrator and Dupin share a house	The Prefect of Police
'The Oval Portrait'	Gothic horror	narrator (unnamed)	(none)	—	Pedro (a servant)
'The Masque of the Red Death'	Gothic horror	Prince Prospero	(none)	—	1000 knights & dames (guests)
'The Pit and the Pendulum'	Gothic horror	Prisoner (unnamed)	(none)	—	General Lasalle (rescuer)
'The Tell-Tale Heart'	Horror	narrator (unnamed)	old man	Narrator lives with and kills the old man	—
'The Black Cat'	Horror	narrator (unnamed)	two black cats (first is named 'Pluto')	Narrator kills first cat; the second gives the narrator away to police	Wife (murdered by the narrator)
'The Premature Burial'	Horror	narrator (unnamed)	(none)	—	Unnamed friend
'The Purloined Letter'	Detective	C. Auguste Dupin	narrator (unnamed)	Narrator and Dupin share a house	The Prefect of Police
'The Cask of Amontillado'	Gothic horror	Montresor	Fortunato	M feels that F has wronged him; M Kills F	Luchresi

INTRODUCTION

During his lifetime, and for much of the time since his death, Edgar Allan Poe (1809–1849) has been regarded as a dark and brooding figure, prone to madness and alcoholism. It is true that Poe was subject to fits of profound depression, which he often dealt with by drinking to excess. It is also the case that, like many great artists and writers, Poe had his quirks and preoccupations – in Poe's case with death and dying.

However, even during his lifetime, Poe was recognised as a writer of skill and talent, although this was not enough to keep him from a state of destitution for several periods during his life. The stories in this selection highlight the two aspects of Poe's writings that have made them enduring literary classics: his creativity and his craftsmanship. Poe was gifted with the creative ability to renew and reinvigorate the form of the short story and the genres (especially the Gothic) in which he wrote. Indeed, he is generally acknowledged as the creator of the detective story.

Poe's short stories represent the best of his literary output. They have withstood the test of time, and continue to perplex and entertain readers. They can be enjoyed on many levels: the more you read these stories, the more you will find in them. The challenge is to look beyond the dark, macabre exterior, in order to explore the underlying themes and motifs. During his life, Poe was often deliberately misleading about himself and his work. Were we to tell him that we were about to undertake a detailed study of his stories, he might well have replied as the narrator of 'The Black Cat' begins his tale:

> For the most wild, yet most homely narrative which I am about to pen, I neither expect nor solicit belief. Mad indeed would I be to expect it … (p.390)

In fact, Poe's tales are not wild, although they explore extreme and seemingly uncontrollable psychological states; the stories themselves are sophisticated, controlled and highly crafted. Nor are they homely, although they are often set in the comfortable homes of the middle- and upper-classes; these tales are exceptional, fascinating and disconcerting. And no matter how much he might have tried to convince us otherwise, Poe was certainly not mad.

BACKGROUND & CONTEXT

Poe's need to make money

The stories examined here were all published for the first time between roughly 1838 and 1845. At this time, Poe was in his early thirties, and had been trying to make a living as a writer and editor since leaving the West Point military academy in 1830. These stories should therefore be seen in the light of this professional context. The need to make money helped Poe to determine the type of story he needed to write, as he earned his income solely from the wages he was paid for working at various magazines and journals, and from the stories and articles he sold to those journals.

In a letter written in 1835 to the editor of the monthly journal *Southern Literary Messenger,* Poe explained what he thought was necessary to attract readers. In particular, he said success came from printing stories like his own 'Berenice' – stories that in general contained:

> The ludicrous heightened into the grotesque: the fearful coloured into the horrible: the witty exaggerated into the burlesque: the singular wrought out into the strange and mystical. (Buranelli 1961, p.24)

Not long after this, Poe became editor of the *Southern Literary Messenger*. Under his tenure, subscriptions increased seven-fold, from 500 to 3,500 copies. He had similar success when he was an editor at *Graham's Magazine* between 1841 and 1842, when subscriptions increased eight-fold, from 5,000 to 40,000. This is clear evidence that Poe knew what readers wanted, and his own stories reflect the popular taste of his time.

Poe's personal life

It is certainly true that Edgar Allan Poe lived a dramatic life, one in which events often seemed to conspire against him. Born in 1809, Poe was dead by the age of forty, having lived much of his life in poverty. Reconstructing

Poe's life is a difficult task, as he was often guilty of obfuscation with regard to his personal circumstances. Examples of this include falsely claiming he travelled to Greece and St Petersburg, while concealing the fact of his period of service in the army. Poe liked to assume the persona of the well-travelled poet: mysterious, passionate and misunderstood. While not altogether a lie, the truth is that Poe was hardworking and conscientious throughout his life.

Poe had some inner demons, however. His parents were both dead before he was two, and he was fostered to a family named 'Allan' (the source of his middle name). He was by all accounts greatly attached to his foster mother, but fell out with his foster father, who eventually refused to have any contact with Poe. In 1827, Sarah Royster, with whom he was in love, was forced to marry another man. The woman he eventually married in 1836, his cousin Virginia Clemm, died in 1847, while Poe was reportedly so poor that he could not afford firewood to heat the house. Many of Poe's relationships with women were to end sadly.

Poe suffered ill fortune professionally throughout his life, which was the main reason for the impoverished circumstances in which he often found himself. Typical of his fortunes was his forced departure from the *Southern Literary Messenger* – which enjoyed great success under Poe's editorship – partly as a result of resentment from the owner, TW White, at Poe's success. Poe moved from one magazine or newspaper to another, was never able to find secure, lasting employment, and was forced to live hand-to-mouth for much of his life. Poe was also prone to depression and emotional panic. Compounding this were his problems with gambling and drinking: while not a constant feature of his life, they frequently returned to haunt him.

The personal problems Poe experienced throughout his life are reflected in his work, and are an important source of his themes and imagery. Many of his characters exhibit a darker side, or are caused to suffer, and Poe is consistently convincing in his descriptions of personal torment, madness and misfortune. We can understand this as being in large part the result of personal experiences, on which Poe was able to draw in portraying such extreme personal and mental states.

GENRE, STRUCTURE & STYLE

Genre

The two main genres used by Poe in these stories are those of Gothic horror and the detective story. In both genres, Poe's work has been extremely influential and provides examples that are widely read and admired.

Gothic tales of horror

In 1764, roughly seventy years before Poe wrote these short stories, Horace Walpole's novel *The Castle of Otranto* was published. This was the first novel in what would become the genre of 'Gothic' or 'Gothic horror' fiction. This genre now includes canonical novels such as Emily Brontë's *Wuthering Heights* (1847), Robert Louis Stevenson's *The Strange Case of Dr Jekyll and Mr Hyde* (1886) and Bram Stoker's *Dracula* (1897). Ten of the twelve Poe stories discussed in this guide can be categorised as Gothic horror stories, or horror stories strongly influenced by the Gothic mode.

The Gothic genre arose in response to social changes, in particular to developments in science. During the 1700s when *The Castle of Otranto* was published, there was an increasing emphasis on science and scientific methodology, and especially on the value of 'reason'. This emphasis on reason included the idea that everything, from the way people lived their lives to the workings of the natural world, operated according to logical laws that could be discovered and understood. This idea even became accepted in religious thinking and teaching. In sermons throughout Europe at the time, God was often conceived of as akin to a 'divine watchmaker', while the world and everything in it were portrayed as being like the mechanism of a watch, waiting to be understood by humanity.

Some people, however, felt that not everything was explainable in such rational terms. They began to be nostalgic for an idealised past, such as the Middle Ages, when people thought that not everything could be explained or known, and 'magic' or the 'supernatural' were sometimes considered to be the forces behind events and phenomena.

The Gothic genre began as an expression of this nostalgic desire. In the traditional Gothic tale, mysterious events and supernatural occurrences play a key part. Typical features of Gothic tales, which we can see in Poe's stories, include manifestations of the supernatural – such as corpses risen from the dead, demons and other monsters, the double or doppelgänger, and hereditary curses. Other common elements include striking images and descriptions of madness, disease, death and decay.

The name 'Gothic' also refers to an ornate style of medieval architecture, and architecture is often an integral feature of Gothic tales. The importance of Gothic architecture in Poe's stories is discussed further in the Style section below.

Poe's use of the Gothic

It is important to understand that the stories of Poe represent a reinterpretation and progression of the Gothic genre. While Poe's stories incorporate many typical features of the Gothic, there are also some crucial differences. In particular, Poe did not share the traditional Gothic interest in the supernatural; his short stories replace the *supernatural* with the *psychological*. Instead of ghosts, witches and mystical curses, Poe's characters tend to be afflicted with psychological disorders, congenital diseases and 'inner demons'.

Detective stories

Many literary historians agree that with the story 'The Murders in the Rue Morgue', Poe created the detective story. Poe wrote two more stories featuring the amateur sleuth, C. Auguste Dupin, as well as other stories featuring similar 'detective' characters and plots. The detective story is relatively straightforward, and has changed little since Poe wrote what remains one of the best examples of the genre.

The two central characters in the classic detective story are a gifted amateur detective character and an assistant who is methodical but not so talented. The detective and their assistant invariably work outside official channels, solving crimes and mysteries that police detectives and inspectors are unable to solve. In inventing this scenario, Poe created a convention for the detective genre that other famous crime writers have followed almost exactly. Sir Arthur Conan Doyle used Sherlock Holmes and his friend Watson to aid the hapless Inspector Lestrade; and Agatha Christie used her character Hercule Poirot, with the help of Hastings, to aid Inspector Japp.

Structure: Poe's ideal short story

By the time Poe published these stories in the late 1830s and early 1840s, the short story format was already flourishing. Notable for their short stories during this period were the French writer Honoré de Balzac and American authors Washington Irving and Nathaniel Hawthorne. Poe was familiar with the works of these and other writers, as he had worked as a critic, analysing short stories, novels and poems. It was partly through his knowledge and understanding of the work of his contemporaries that Poe was able to take the short story structure to new heights.

In 1842, in what is now a well-known review of Nathaniel Hawthorne's *Twice-Told Tales*, Poe outlined what he thought the ideal structure of a short story should be (see pp.519–28 for this review). In particular, Poe wrote that the author should have a 'certain unique or single *effect*' that they were trying to achieve, and the author's story should then combine 'such events as may best aid him in establishing this preconceived effect' (p.522). Poe stressed that: 'In the whole composition there should be no word written, of which the tendency, direct or indirect, is not to the one pre-established design' (p.522).

In other words, for Poe, a good short story had a single overriding theme or idea, and every element of the story should contribute to this theme. If information was included that was not strictly necessary for achieving the key 'effect', the story could (in Poe's opinion) be considered a failure. Poe's stories are structurally consistent and adhere to this rule.

Style: a poetic understanding of language

The ornate and complex style of Poe's short stories owes much to his serious and sustained commitment to writing poetry. While his poems are less highly regarded than his stories, some of them were nonetheless popular and remain well known – 'The Raven' is the most obvious example (pp.73–8). Poe's in-depth working knowledge of poetic skills and techniques clearly influenced the way he used language in his stories.

Maximising the impact of words

In particular, Poe understood the need to make every word count, as space is limited in both poems and short stories. This is evident, for instance, in 'The Pit and the Pendulum', as in the passage: 'Shaking in every limb, I groped my way back to the wall; resolving there to perish rather than risk the terrors of the wells' (p.373). Here, Poe's choice of certain words heightens our appreciation of the prisoner's feelings of desperation and disorientation. The prisoner does not just 'feel' his way back to the wall; he 'gropes' his way back. This latter word conveys a much stronger sense of uncertainty and desperation. Additionally, the prisoner expects not simply to 'die', or even 'succumb', but to 'perish'. This word conveys a tragic finality to the prisoner's situation, a sense that he will not just die but disappear entirely. Poe thus gives this passage maximum meaning and impact through the careful selection and expert control of language.

Lyrical qualities of language

Poe's experience as a poet also enhanced the lyrical quality of his prose writing. This is the sense of written words having a musical quality and flowing like a song. Reading aloud the last sentence of 'The Fall of the House of Usher' (p.238) demonstrates this quality of Poe's writing. The sentence is long, with the clauses (groups of words) separated by dashes rather than commas. This gives the sense of one thought or observation flowing rapidly into the next without pause. Simply by listening to the cadences (rise and fall) of the language, and the way the sentence flows increasingly quickly with the words becoming more dramatic, the reader gains a sense of the House of Usher collapsing, slowly at first, and then with increasing rapidity into the murky waters of the tarn.

Style: first-person narration

Poe's use of first-person narrators is crucial to the effects these stories achieve, and to the construction of complexity in characters even when they have little or no interaction with others. Normally these interactions and relationships give us a deeper understanding of the characters' personalities and values. However, Poe uses first-person narration to depict events from the perspective of a central character, giving us an insight not just into the world of that character but also into the workings of the character's mind.

Key point

As readers, we must accept that the narration will not always be reliable. Nevertheless, by noting the discrepancies in a character's narration, it is possible to build a profile of that character's true hopes and fears, even when they attempt to hide these from others.

A brief and obvious example of determining the characteristics of an unreliable narrator is provided in 'The Tell-Tale Heart'. We know not to rely on the narrator's version of events as absolute truth, because he tells us that he can hear a dead heart beating. This obvious untruth reveals the narrator's state of delusion and paranoia, and so conveys a psychological truth on a deeper level than does his material or physical circumstances.

Style: architectural imagery

An important group of images and symbols throughout Poe's stories can be found in the descriptions of buildings that the characters live in or visit. Specifically, these buildings are examples of Gothic architecture – ornate, overbearing, dark, brooding structures, which powerfully convey a sense of mood and atmosphere.

The most obvious reference to Gothic architecture as a device for conveying mood occurs in 'The Oval Portrait', in which the narrator's reference to the author Anne Radcliffe at once suggests both the chateau's architectural style and the tone and genre of the story. Interestingly, on a deeper level, this allusion also leads us to question the seriousness of the author's intent. Poe is clearly mocking the Gothic genre, and particularly the description of overly elaborate, excessively brooding architecture, which is one of its most typical features. Perhaps Poe suggests here that the symbolism of such architecture is overly simplistic. There is no doubt, however, that he found the highly recognisable nature of these symbols to be extremely useful and effective, as the classic images of Gothic architecture are often deployed in his own tales. They are often closely linked with the themes of illness, death, madness and entrapment – see the Themes, Ideas & Values section for detailed discussions of these.

STORY-BY-STORY ANALYSIS

'Berenice' (pp.152–61)

Summary: *Egæus, who was born in the family library and has spent most of his life there, agrees to marry his cousin, Berenice; he becomes obsessed with her teeth; when she dies, Egæus digs up her body while in a trance, and removes her teeth.*

Translation of epigraph: 'My companions told me I might find some little alleviation of my misery, in visiting the grave of my beloved'.

Egæus has had an unusual upbringing: he has lived his entire life in the library of his mansion. The influences of the library on Egæus are those of 'monastic thought and erudition' (p.153) – Egæus represents intellectualism, and specifically its negative aspects. He reads about ideas and concepts, and considers them in an abstract way. He is completely isolated from the world, with no way of understanding the reality of what he reads about.

Egæus confirms this when he observes: 'In the strange anomaly of my existence, feelings with me, *had never been* of the heart, and my passions *always were* of the mind' (p.157). Egæus cannot experience emotions in the normal manner; nor is he able to relate to objects and people in the usual way. This aspect of his character leads to his downfall when he develops an obsession with Berenice's teeth. He dwells on her teeth so long and intensely that eventually he 'seriously believed *que tous ses dents etaient des idées. Des idées!*' ('that all her teeth were ideas. Ideas!', p.159). Once Egæus conceives of Berenice's teeth as ideas, they enter the world of the intellect and Egæus is able to love them as he has loved nothing else.

The seeds for what is to come are laid when Egæus describes the symptoms of Berenice's regressive disease. Consistent with the representation of illness in Poe's stories, the affliction described is vague and debilitating. Notably, however, one of Berenice's symptoms is a trance-like state 'very nearly resembling positive dissolution' (p.154) – a state that prepares us for Berenice's premature burial.

When Egæus learns that Berenice has 'been seized with epilepsy' (p.160) and is soon to be buried, we have every reason to suspect the worst will happen. This is confirmed when the servants, hearing a scream, rush to the 'violated grave' and discover 'a disfigured body enshrouded, yet still breathing, still palpitating, *still alive!*' (p.161) There is a lingering effect to the conclusion of 'Berenice', when we realise that Egæus has removed Berenice's teeth while she was still alive, and then left her, confirming his complete detachment from conventional feelings and relationships.

Q Does Egæus' illness adequately explain or excuse his actions?

'The Fall of the House of Usher' (pp.216–38)

Summary: *The unnamed narrator visits his friend, Roderick Usher, to help him through a time of illness; Roderick becomes mentally and physically unstable; the narrator flees as the House of Usher collapses, killing Roderick and his twin sister, Madeline.*

Translation of epigraph: 'His heart is a suspended lute; as soon as it is touched, it resounds'.

Some of the classic symbols of the Gothic genre are evident in this story. The first and most obvious of these is the imagery of Gothic architecture and death, especially in the depiction of the House of Usher. The house symbolises the Usher family, and this symbolism is reinforced as the story progresses. Roderick strengthens the narrator's own feelings of gloom with his ideas about the 'influence' of the 'family mansion ... over his spirit' (p.223). The house is dark and foreboding; it makes the narrator uneasy, and Roderick has the same effect on him.

The narrator finds his childhood friend to be wasting away, attaining a 'cadaverousness of complexion' (p.221). But the worst part of Usher's disease is the unreasoning fear that has come to dominate his thoughts. Eventually this fear also overwhelms the narrator and becomes the central element in the story as a whole. The role that fear plays in the minds of the two male characters is discussed further in the Characters & Relationships section.

Key point

In this and other Gothic horror stories by Poe, the fear arising from the unconscious part of the mind will always overwhelm the rational, conscious part of the mind.

The metaphor of the house as an embodiment of the Usher family is extended in the final scenes of the story. Roderick and his sister symbolise the diseased and dying mind and soul of the Ushers, while the house symbolises its body. Finally the metaphor is completed when the house collapses as the last of the Ushers die.

Q How reliable is the narrator's version of events in this story?

'William Wilson' (pp.238–61)

Summary: *William Wilson is given to criminal and wicked acts; he is pursued by his conscience, which has taken the form of an exact replica of himself, and which he eventually kills.*

'William Wilson' examines the psychology of the protagonist (leading character), showing the way guilt motivates his actions. The story makes use of a figure from northern European folklore, the double or doppelgänger. The doppelgänger is a look-alike or exact double of an individual. Typically in folklore the doppelgänger, who casts no shadow and speaks with a whisper, is one's 'dark double' or 'evil twin'. Doppelgängers were thought to be the harbingers and even perpetrators of bad luck or dire circumstances. William Wilson's double, the person with the same name and visage who reappears whenever Wilson is about to commit a villainous act, is an allegorical figure: that is, he is not a distinct individual or character, but represents an abstract idea or quality. In this story, Wilson's double represents his conscience.

Finally Wilson grows tired of his duplicate always appearing 'to disturb those actions, which, if fully carried out, might have resulted in bitter mischief' (p.258). As in folklore, the doppelgänger's appearance is a portent of bad luck for its original. Wilson engages his double in a sword fight and kills him. However, upon doing so, Wilson has the impression that he is looking in a mirror and seeing himself 'pale and dabbled in blood' (p.261). The symbolism of the mirror is clear: Wilson has killed an aspect of his own personality – his conscience. Thus, his double tells Wilson that although his body remains alive, he is now 'dead to the World, to Heaven and to Hope!' (p.261).

Q How does Poe use symbols and symbolism in this story? Identify two or three symbols and explain what they stand for.

Q Is 'William Wilson' simply a horror story? Why/why not?

'The Murders in the Rue Morgue' (pp.272–313)

Summary: *The narrator meets Monsieur C. Auguste Dupin, who has remarkable analytical skills. After they move into a house together, Dupin solves a gruesome double murder that has baffled the Paris Police.*

In this story Poe combines most of the elements that the best detective stories would later use. In particular, Poe creates a trio of characters who play unique, interlocking roles. Firstly, Dupin is the brilliant but eccentric amateur detective. The key aspect of this character is that he notices things that others do not, and understands how they can be interpreted as clues. An example of this occurs when Dupin uses the testimony of the witnesses to understand that whoever murdered Madame L'Espanaye and her daughter did not speak any language at all. The clue (that all the witnesses heard what they thought was speech and assumed that it was simply a language they could not understand) is there in the text for all to see. Yet it takes a person of special analytical ability, such as Dupin, to understand the true meaning and significance of this clue.

The second important character is the narrator. In Poe's tale, the narrator is unnamed, which is symbolic: the narrator represents the common person of ordinary intelligence, who does not possess the analytical genius of Dupin. Poe uses the narrator to create the impression that the brilliant insights of the detective – Dupin – must be put into terms others will understand. This act of 'translation' helps to reinforce the idea that Dupin is a genius. For example, Dupin must explain to the narrator the reason why the police could not determine a motive for the killings, adding that the apparent lack of motive helped him to solve the case, whereas it only confounded the police (pp.292–3). In explaining his logic to the narrator – and therefore to the reader as well – Dupin confirms his analytical superiority.

The third important character is the Prefect of Police. The Prefect and the Parisian Police are unable to solve the crime, and Dupin must do it for them – even though they are professionals and he is an amateur. This adds drama to the story, giving it greater narrative interest than a story generated simply by a character recounting how they solved a particular crime.

Q Using textual examples, explain how Dupin is shown to have superior analytical skills.

'The Oval Portrait' (pp.355–9)

Summary: *A wounded man and his servant take shelter in an empty chateau. While in bed, the wounded man sees, then reads about an extremely lifelike portrait, the painting of which led to the subject's death.*

'The Oval Portrait' epitomises Poe's approach to writing a short story (see 'Structure: Poe's ideal short story' in the Genre, Structure & Style section). It is a tale that can provoke much thought, despite its particularly short length. It does so by grabbing the attention of the reader using a minimum of information. In fact, its omission of details about the characters is part of what provokes reader interest. We have an unnamed narrator, with an unnamed valet – suggesting the narrator has wealth and social status. The narrator is 'desperately wounded' (p.355), although he does not say how, which is intriguing.

The characters arrive at an abandoned castle in the mountains, which the narrator describes by referring to 'the fancy of Mrs. Radcliffe' (p.355). This is a reference to Anne Radcliffe, a famous author of Gothic novels from the late 1700s. Poe thus gives us a sense not just of the kind of building the castle is – by comparing it to the dark, mysterious castles or monasteries in remote locales that are prevalent in Radcliffe's novels – but also of the genre the story belongs to.

Another layer of complexity is added when the narrator reads about the painting of the portrait hanging in his room. He discovers that, as the artist painted his subject over a period of many weeks, she gradually grew weak and ill as the act of painting somehow drew the life out of her. This story-within-a-story is a cautionary moral tale about the value of art compared to life. The artist, gazing on his finished masterpiece, cries: 'This is indeed *Life* itself!' (p.359), implying that his artistic creation is the equal of life. However, as the painter turns from his painting, he sees that his beloved has literally given her life to enable the painting to be created.

The maiden's gradual death is thus an allegory for (that is, a parallel story about) the gap between art and life. While the painter has created an idealised version of his beloved's beauty, which he believes is timeless and will last forever, it is without life. Further, the painting required the beauty of the girl in order even to exist. While the beauty of the painting may defy time, the girl's beauty is mortal and cannot live forever.

Q What elements of the story can be seen as symbols, or as allegorical? For instance, consider the roles of the chateau; the candelabrum; the portrait; the girl's death; the actions of the painter/husband.

Q What techniques does Poe use to capture the reader's interest and heighten the suspense in this story? Give examples to support your answer.

'The Masque of the Red Death' (pp.359–66)

Summary: *Prince Prospero summons a thousand knights and dames and retires to an abbey to escape from a plague; during a masked ball, the plague takes human form and enters the abbey, killing all those within.*

'The Masque of the Red Death' contains several plays on words, which suggest the idea that deeper layers of meaning can often lie beneath surface appearances. Prospero's lands are being destroyed by the 'Red

Death', a reference to the Black Death, or bubonic plague, which swept Europe in the Middle Ages; the difference in colour suggests that we are in an exotic location, removed from medieval Europe.

Another play on words is the name of the protagonist – Prince Prospero. Unlike the famous Prospero from Shakespeare's play *The Tempest*, who lives in exile on an island with only his daughter and two servants for company, Prince Prospero has surrounded himself with a thousand people inside a fortress. Interestingly, one of Prospero's servants in *The Tempest*, the deformed Caliban, curses his master with the words: 'The red plague rid you/For learning me your language' (I.ii.336–8) – and Poe's Prospero is indeed killed by the 'red plague'.

Perhaps the most important play on words is in the title. 'Masque' is a reference to both 'Masquerade' – the masked ball thrown by Prince Prospero – and the 'mask' that the revellers think is being worn by a guest, but which actually turns out to belong to the Red Death. This play on words is significant because it draws attention to what the Prince and his guests are really doing – attempting to 'mask' and hide the nature of their reality. This is why they cannot recognise death when they see it, but mistake the costume and mask as simply another disguise: they believe their lives of power and privilege can protect them from the plague, and that death can be kept outside the walls of the abbey. However, the 'mask' worn by the Red Death signifies not an illusion, but reality, which is revealed as soon as the 'grave-cerements and corpse-like mask' are removed (p.366).

Q Is 'The Masque of the Red Death' simply a horror story, or is there a deeper meaning? Explain your response.

Q What contrasting symbolism does the author use in the words and images of this story?

'The Pit and the Pendulum' (pp.366–84)

Summary: *An unnamed prisoner is sentenced to death by the Spanish Inquisition in Toledo. He is then placed in a cell where he undergoes a series of macabre tortures before he is rescued by the French General Lasalle.*

Translation of epigraph: 'Here the impious clamour of the torturers / Insatiate, fed its rage for innocent blood. / Now happy is the land, destroyed the pit of horror, / And where grim death stalked, life and health are revealed.'

In this story Poe demonstrates his ability to convey a character's mental state. His precise use of language means that the reader gains a powerful sense not just of the prisoner's circumstances, but also of his state of fear. For example, when the prisoner lies in darkness after being thrown into the cell he trembles 'convulsively' and thrusts his arms 'wildly' into the darkness (p.370). These words indicate that the prisoner's actions are almost uncontrollable, and that his situation is extreme.

Poe uses a number of techniques to focus our attention on the prisoner's state of mind. These include alliteration, such as the repeated 's' sound in the 'sweep', 'hissing' and 'descent' of the pendulum (p.378). Another technique is anaphora (a repeated word or phrase at the start of clauses), such as the repetition of 'then' to signal the gradual recovery of recent memories:

> Then a pause in which all is blank. Then again sound, and motion ... Then the mere consciousness of existence ... Then, very suddenly, *thought* ...Then a strong desire to lapse into insensibility. Then a rushing revival of soul and a successful effort to move. (p.369)

At times the prisoner struggles against his predicament, such as when he first realises the sharpened pendulum is gradually swinging towards him. However, by giving in to wilder emotions and madness, the prisoner cannot ease his suffering. Only when he becomes 'suddenly calm' (p.377) is he able to think of a way to escape. In this way we can see the story as showing a struggle not merely against unjust suffering, but also against the forces of fear and madness. In this story, as in 'The Murders in the Rue Morgue', Poe suggests that reason can – if exerted powerfully enough – sometimes overcome the less rational forces of fear and horror.

Q How does Poe create suspense in this story?

'The Tell-Tale Heart' (pp.384–9)

Summary: *The narrator is obsessed with the eye of an old man with whom he lives. He kills the old man and hides the body under the floorboards. When the police arrive, the narrator thinks he can hear the beating of the old man's dead heart, and confesses.*

This story has a similar plot and themes to 'The Black Cat'. In both stories the narrator's obsession compels them to commit a crime, only to find that their guilt leads them to give themselves away.

Key point

This tale explores the relationship between obsession – and the actions that arise from it – and guilt.

The narrator begins by assuring the reader that he is not mad but sane, and that the reason he can hear 'all things in the heaven and in the earth' (p.384) is because of a disease that has sharpened his senses. The narrator also tries to demonstrate his sanity by telling us that he spent an hour each night opening the door to the old man's room just enough to poke his head and a lantern in, then asking: 'would a madman have been so wise as this?' (p.385). The answer, of course, is 'what sane person would do this?' By trying to prove his sanity, he demonstrates his madness.

When the police come to investigate a cry overheard by a neighbour, the narrator thinks he can hear *'a low, dull quick sound'* (p.389) – which he believes is the dead man's heart. His guilt makes him nervous, a feeling that is intensified when he thinks that the police can also hear the sound, and finally the narrator's 'agony' leads him to confess. Of course, the 'Tell-Tale Heart' that gives him away is his own guilty heart beating heavily in his chest.

Q How does Poe convey the narrator's mental state?

Q Is the narrator convincing in his argument that he is not mad? Explain why/why not.

'The Black Cat' (pp.390–401)

Summary: *A man who is initially gentle and loves animals changes, becoming a violent alcoholic who kills his favourite pet cat; he then kills his wife; a second black cat has been trapped with his wife's body and reveals its whereabouts to police.*

The plot and themes of this story are similar to those of 'The Tell-Tale Heart'. However, the narrator of 'The Black Cat' provides a more detailed account of his personal history, and has a different motive for relating his tale. Whereas the narrator of 'The Tell-Tale Heart' is convinced of his sanity and is merely explaining the reason for his arrest, the narrator of 'The Black Cat' is no longer convinced that he is of sound mind. He relates the events of the story in order that 'some intellect may be found which will reduce my phantasm to the common-place' (p.390).

The narrator is attempting to explain how he has changed from being 'noted for the docility and humanity of [his] disposition' (p.390) to 'wretched beyond the wretchedness of mere Humanity' (p.397). He blames this change on 'the Fiend Intemperance' – that is, on alcoholism. Moreover, once the narrator has begun to act violently, his deeds gradually become more extreme. Poe thus depicts the psychology of someone becoming progressively more deranged.

On one occasion, the narrator, in a rage, cuts out the eye of his pet cat, Pluto. But this act only makes him angrier, and he goes on to hang the cat – knowing that in doing so he is 'committing a sin' that would 'jeopardize [his] immortal soul' (p.393). In this way, a self-perpetuating cycle of violence and guilt begins. The narrator becomes mean and cruel to those around him. These acts of cruelty make him feel remorse, which he finds painful. In order to punish someone for the pain he feels, he inflicts more harm on others. And so the pattern continues.

This cycle culminates when the narrator kills his wife for interfering when he attempts to harm the second cat. The story then concludes in an ambiguous fashion when the cat alerts the police to the location of the corpse. On the one hand, there is the implication that divine retribution has been achieved, since the cat might be the reincarnation of Pluto, returned to punish the narrator. On the other hand, the narrator, in his nervous guilt at the crime he has committed, dwells too long in the cellar with the police. He is responsible for the police being there long enough to hear the cat – suggesting that it is nothing more than his guilt that leads to his evil actions being discovered and punished.

Q Which events lead the central character to doubt his sanity? Is he right to do so?

'The Premature Burial' (pp.413–30)

Summary: *The narrator suffers from catalepsy and is obsessed with premature burial; eventually he overcomes his obsession and illness.*

In this story, Poe once again dwells on the power of the subconscious mind. The narrator's fear of being buried alive dominates his thoughts and has made him ill. His catalepsy (loss of sensation and ability to move) is an obsessive disorder: his obsession is so strong it manifests itself uncontrollably in his behaviour.

Poe takes an interesting approach to the narrative structure of this story. The first section of the story is in the style of journalism or reportage. The narrator begins with a serious and believable tone, recounting what he assures us are true accounts of people being buried alive. Halfway through, however, the narrative style switches from reportage to that of a reflection on events in the narrator's life. The tone becomes less detached and more personal. The narrator is thus hoping to reinforce the truth of his own tale by prefacing it with other, similar tales that have the appearance of 'fact' rather than 'fiction'.

A second shift in style occurs when the narrator is sheltering in the narrow bunk of a river boat. On waking up he fears that all his preparations to avoid a premature burial have been for nothing. Just when he is about to give in to his panic he hears voices:

> "Hillo! hillo, there!" said a gruff voice in reply.
> "What the devil's the matter now?" said a second.
> "Get out o' that!" said a third.
> "What do you mean by yowling in that ere kind of style, like a cattymount?" said a fourth ... (p.428)

The humorous style of these voices contrasts strongly with the rest of the story. The narrative to this point has consisted of a serious discussion of catalepsy and ghastly visions, written in precise, learned language. However, suddenly the accents and vocabulary of the boat's crew inject humour into the narrative, and break the spell that the narrator's fear had cast over both him and the reader.

The story ends with a final twist, as the narrator warns us that we should be careful what we read, and not take too seriously tales of horror that are obviously untrue, including tales *'such as this'* (p.429). This calls into question all that we have read, including the supposedly 'true' accounts of premature burial. The conclusion also raises the possibility that the narrator has taken such stories too seriously, and that his 'illness' has in fact been caused by his obsession with the idea of premature burial rather than by any underlying reality.

Q What methods does Poe use to make readers take the story more seriously?

Q Is the story a serious or a comic tale? Explain your answer.

'The Purloined Letter' (pp.430–51)

Summary: *Dupin and the narrator are visited by the Prefect of Police, who is baffled by a case involving a stolen letter. The Prefect describes the investigation; Dupin deduces where the letter must be, and retrieves it.*

Translation of epigraph: 'Nothing is more hateful to wisdom than excessive cunning'.

Like 'The Murders in the Rue Morgue', this story also features the amateur detective C. Auguste Dupin. Its central point, which Dupin relates to the narrator, is that the Police only looked where they thought a letter would most likely be hidden, based on their own experiences and conventional methods. In studying the Minister D——, and by thinking as *he* would think in order to locate the letter, Dupin (and Poe) demonstrates the value of using reason and logic to think beyond one's own dominant paradigm and assumptions.

Q What is Dupin's opinion of the Prefect of Police? Use examples from the text to support your answer.

Q Do you think Dupin's method for solving the problem is sound, or does he just take a lucky guess? Why?

'The Cask of Amontillado' (pp.496–503)

Summary: *In order to exact revenge for insult and injuries, Montresor lures Fortunato to the cellar of his home, where he seals Fortunato alive in a tomb.*

This tale is another example of Poe demonstrating in practice his theory of how short stories should be written. It is tightly plotted, with no loose ends. There is no superfluous information, yet the story's setting, characters and action are conveyed in enough detail to achieve the author's desired 'effect'.

The story deals with revenge and pride. Montresor is convinced he has suffered as a result of the 'thousand injuries of Fortunato' and because Fortunato has 'ventured upon insult' (p.496). His conviction that this is justification for revenge makes Montresor calm when it comes to deceiving Fortunato and pretending to be his friend. Much of the dramatic tension in this story is created by the reader's knowing something that Fortunato does not – that he is going to die. We can therefore see double meanings, where Fortunato cannot. This use of dramatic irony adds an edge of chilling suspense to the story.

Thus, when the 'nitre' exacerbates Fortunato's cough and Fortunato comments that 'I shall not die of a cough' (p.499), we, like Montresor, understand that there is a double meaning. The cough is not going to kill Fortunato, but Montresor is. A similar situation occurs when Montresor tells Fortunato that they should return to the surface because: 'Your health is precious ... You are a man to be missed' (pp.498–9). Fortunato takes these words at face value. But again, we know they are heavy with irony: Fortunato's health is not precious to Montresor, nor will Montresor miss Fortunato in the slightest.

Not all double meanings are immediately obvious; but when the real meaning of a word or expression does become clear, the effect is even more chilling. For example, when Fortunato asks Montresor (who is unfamiliar with the sign Fortunato has just made) if he is a mason, Montresor replies that he is, and shows Fortunato a trowel. Although Montresor's response is initially confusing, we realise later that while Fortunato was referring to the international order of Freemasons, Montresor was implying that he would be engaging in some masonry when he constructs a wall to trap Fortunato in the catacombs.

Although Fortunato is the victim of Montresor's scheme, his pride leads the reader to be, rather like Montresor, unsympathetic to Fortunato's fate. When Montresor implies that Luchresi might also be able to test his Amontillado, Fortunato's pride and greed lead him to insist on being taken immediately to the cask. Later, Montresor only has to mention the name 'Luchresi' for Fortunato to proclaim: 'He is an ignoramus' (p.501). In this way, Poe suggests the negative effects of excessive pride, and makes it difficult to approve of or sympathise with either character in this story.

Q How does Poe create suspense through his use of language and dialogue? Give examples to support your answer.

Q How sympathetically does Poe portray the characters in this story? Give examples to support your answer.

CHARACTERS & RELATIONSHIPS

Poe's short stories can present challenges for the reader in the analysis of characters, resulting both from the manner in which they are characterised, and the way in which they relate to each other. As has been discussed in the Genre, Structure & Style section, Poe had clear, well-developed ideas about how short stories should be written. He felt that they should contain nothing that did not contribute to the 'effect' – such as the creation of a strong mood or feeling – that the author was trying to achieve. In this conception of the short story, the development of complex, realistic characters and relationships is not strictly necessary for the story to achieve its intended effect. Stories such as 'The Oval Portrait' and 'The Masque of the Red Death' are clear illustrations of this principle.

Poe therefore did not construct characters as fully realised or realistic individuals. However, he did use characters as a means of exploring some unusual and extreme psychological states – often relating to the overwhelming experiences of certain emotions (such as fear or guilt) or, in some cases, the complete absence of conventional feelings and relationships.

Solitary characters

Looking at the Character Table at the start of this guide, we can see there are four stories in which there is really only one significant character, on whom the story centres and who has no major relationship. Two other stories, 'William Wilson' and 'The Black Cat', do contain another major character but the narrator is of principal interest. The use of the first-person narrative voice in most of these stories is crucial both to our understanding of these solitary individuals and to the creation of mood and tension (see 'Style: first-person narrators' in the Genre, Structure & Style section).

Narrator of 'The Oval Portrait'

Key quote

> 'That I now saw aright I could not and would not doubt ...' (p.357)

The susceptibility of the conscious mind to the power of the unconscious is at the centre of this mysterious character. At first this story simply appears to be an unnerving tale about a mysterious painting. However, on closer inspection, the narrator himself is of interest. An intriguing question to ask is whether he has imagined the oval portrait. When he comes to the chateau he is injured, and then he reads long into the night. The oval portrait of the title only becomes visible when the narrator, 'with difficulty', moves the candelabrum (p.356). At this point his valet is sleeping, and the narrator is tired and injured, so there is no-one to confirm that this painting is in fact there, and that the narrator is not in delirium, simply imagining the whole thing.

When the narrator assures us that he has gone from being in a dreamy stupor to being startled 'at once into waking life' (p.357), it is as if he is trying to convince himself as much as the reader. One possible reading, then, is that his new state of alertness is the result of a dream, rather than of being suddenly wide awake in the middle of the night. The story invites us to consider the prospect that the mentally and physically exhausted narrator has been overcome by his dreams.

Prince Prospero

Key quote

> 'But the Prince Prospero was happy and dauntless and sagacious. When his dominions were half depopulated, he summoned to his presence a thousand hale and light-hearted friends from among the knights and dames of his court, and with these retired to the deep seclusion of one of his castellated abbeys.' (p.359)

Despite the fact that he is named, unlike many of Poe's characters, Prince Prospero is perhaps the least well-defined major character. We only gain hints of what he is like by making inferences from the text. This is in part because Poe deviates from an otherwise standard technique, using third-person narration rather than first-person. While the omniscient voice of the narrator makes the moral aspect of this tale straightforward, it also means we have less information about Prince Prospero, as we are not seeing events from his perspective. Instead we must judge him solely by his actions. In a time of death and plague, for example, he summons 'light-hearted friends' (p.359), which indicates that he wishes to surround himself with people who can be happy while many around them are dying.

This is the essence of the Prince's character: he wishes to ignore the death he sees around him, in the forlorn hope that by so doing, he will not succumb to it. Again, the major relationship is internal, because the figure of Death stalking the rooms of the Prince's 'castellated abbey' is a manifestation of what the Prince most fears: the ravages of death by the Red Plague. He and his guests are representative of all people, because who is not afraid of death?

In this sense, the Prince is a sympathetic figure; but he is also a figure of derision and scorn, because he is vain and indifferent to the suffering of others. Prince Prospero believes his wealth and power (the power to make others laugh and dance when they are threatened by the plague) will protect him, but of course they cannot.

The prisoner

Key quotes

'After this I call to mind flatness and dampness; and then all is *madness*—the madness of a memory which busies itself among forbidden things.' (p.369)

'Then a strong desire to lapse into insensibility. Then a rushing revival of soul …' (p.369)

The prisoner of 'The Pit and Pendulum' is of interest by virtue of the fact that he is unique amongst the characters in this selection of Poe's stories. This is for a number of reasons, the first of which is that his suffering has been externally imposed. Unlike most of the other characters, who cause their own problems, the prisoner is being tortured by others. This leads to a second point of difference, which is that, unlike the narrator of 'The Tell-Tale Heart' for example, who gives in to his obsession and to madness, the prisoner struggles against oblivion, both mental and physical.

There is a key point in the text, upon which our understanding of the prisoner's character turns. While lying waiting for the pendulum to descend, the prisoner tells us:

> I prayed—I wearied heaven with my prayer for [the pendulum's] more speedy descent. I grew frantically mad, and struggled to force myself upward against the sweep of the fearful scimitar. And then I fell suddenly calm, and lay smiling at the glittering death, as a child at some rare bauble. (p.377)

From this point, the prisoner starts to think, to devise schemes, and to try to escape from his bonds. This marks a key difference between the prisoner and other characters. He overcomes the madness of his fear – which comes from his subconscious. He turns instead to his conscious mind – the thinking part of his brain. When he does this, he triumphs, and escapes the surcingle (bandage). The story examines the relationship of one part of the prisoner's personality to another, as in the other stories. Unlike in the other stories, though, fear and madness do not overcome him.

Narrator of 'The Tell-Tale Heart' and Montresor

Key quotes

'I loved the old man. He had never wronged me. He had never given me insult ... by degrees—very gradually—I made up my mind to take the life of the old man, and thus rid myself of the eye forever.' ('The Tell-Tale Heart', p.384)

'*At length* I would be avenged; this was a point definitively settled—but the very definitiveness with which it was resolved precluded the idea of risk.' ('The Cask of Amontillado', p.496)

These characters have two central features, which means we can group them together. Firstly, they both display paranoid and obsessive tendencies. And secondly, unlike the narrator of the 'The Black Cat', they do not question the legitimacy of their impulses, or hesitate to act on their obsessions. Both are confessing to their crimes at some point after having committed them. This indicates both the presence of some form of guilt, and also the inability of that guilt to prevent these characters from carrying out their heinous crimes. This is borne out by the fact that, although the stories are told from the point of view of a confession after the fact, neither character seems to be seeking absolution.

Montresor's tale is straightforward, and his motivation obvious: he is simply relating an act of murder, perhaps to a priest on his deathbed, which he believed he was justified in committing. Likewise, the narrator of 'The Tell-Tale Heart' seems more interested in convincing us of his sanity, and of the bizarre circumstances of his capture, than he is in justifying his gruesome actions.

William Wilson and the narrator of 'The Black Cat'

Key quotes

'I grew self-willed, addicted to the wildest caprices, and a prey to the most ungovernable passions.' ('William Wilson', p.239)

'I grew, day by day, more moody, more irritable, more regardless of the feelings of others. I suffered myself to use intemperate language to my wife. At length, I even offered her personal violence.' ('The Black Cat', p.391)

These two characters can be grouped together because, although their personal motivations vary, the nature of the central relationship in which they are engaged is essentially the same. The second William Wilson and the second, unnamed black cat both represent the conscience of the protagonist.

William Wilson does not question his dissolute lifestyle; he is unable to, as he has no conscience of his own. Thus, he is both literally and symbolically running from his own conscience. His fear becomes anger, but this is still the anger of one part of his personality (the part that wants to engage in immoral behaviour whenever it pleases) at another part (which attempts to restrain him from inflicting harm on others). This is illustrated perfectly when Wilson says that his shadow self has 'poor justification' showing up in order to thwart Wilson's 'schemes ... which ... might have resulted in bitter mischief' (p.258).

The narrator of 'The Black Cat' also lives in fear of his conscience, represented by the second black cat, which bore a:

> mark of white hair ... [which] had, at length, assumed a rigorous distinctness of outline. It was now the representation of an object that I shudder to name ... of the GALLOWS! (pp.396–7)

The mark is a visible reminder of the punishment he has inflicted on Pluto. Curiously, the narrator does not indicate whether his wife can also see the outline of the gallows, or whether she has simply noticed the distinctive mark of white hair. The narrator confesses that he 'longed to destroy [the cat] with a blow' (p.396). Like Wilson, he wishes to destroy that part of his personality – his conscience – which prevents him from living comfortably with the terrible deeds he has committed.

These stories thus contain an element of self-awareness on the part of the protagonists, which is absent from the narrator of 'The Tell-Tale Heart'. Both Wilson and the narrator of 'The Black Cat' are aware of guilty consciences that disturb them, and which they wish to silence.

Strong protagonists and weak narrators

The stories 'The Fall of the House of Usher', 'The Murders in the Rue Morgue' and 'The Purloined letter' are linked by a similar relationship between the central characters. In each story, the narrator is a relatively weak individual who is dominated by the more powerful or skilful protagonist.

Key point

In each of these stories the narrator is essentially a cipher: a character who has few features or characteristics of their own, and whose presence is primarily a narrative device to allow the author to tell the story of the stronger central character.

There are many reasons for using a weak narrator and strong central character. The main reason is that it allows the author to tell a story that is essentially about one character; but, by having a second character relate events, the author can include dialogue and conversation between the two characters that would otherwise be impossible.

Roderick Usher and the narrator

Key quote

'... there was a species of mad hilarity in his eyes—an evidently restrained *hysteria* in his whole demeanor.' (p.232)

The narrator of 'The Fall of the House of Usher' remains unnamed, indicating his minor role in the story. The key to understanding the dynamic between the central characters comes when we realise that the narrator, while he stays with Roderick, gradually becomes infected with his friend's debilitating illness, and in particular with the fear from which Roderick claims to suffer.

The narrator's observations, such as that when they are placing Madeline in the vault they do so behind doors of 'massive iron' (p.230), and that her coffin has a lid that they 'screwed down', mean that he has no reason to believe Roderick's fantastic claims about the reincarnation of his dead sister. He also makes other important observations, such as that the tomb was once used to store gunpowder, and still has the reek of the 'combustible substance' (p.230). Additionally, the tomb is lined with copper, an excellent conductor in a storm. These revelations are meant to stand in contrast to Roderick's later version of events, thereby providing the reader with a rational avenue by which Roderick's claims can be both explained and dismissed as the ravings of someone who is clearly deranged.

So when Roderick proclaims that he has buried Madeline alive, that she is somehow 'rending' the lid of her coffin, and that the noises they can hear are not the storm but the sounds of Madeline's 'struggles within the coppered archway of the vault' (p.237), the narrator can have, as we have seen, no reason to believe Roderick's version of events. Upon hearing this, however, the narrator disregards the evidence of his own senses. Madeline, after all, suffered from catalepsy, causing her to go into a trance and appear dead. The narrator is clearly clinging to this fact to justify his belief in Roderick's proclamations. The narrator succumbs to Roderick's vision of terror, demonstrating the supremacy of unconscious terror over conscious rationality. Thus, in relating Roderick's circumstances, the narrator becomes like the character he is seeking to describe.

C. Auguste Dupin and the narrator

Key quote

'"That was the evidence itself," said Dupin, "but it was not the peculiarity of the evidence. You have observed nothing distinctive. Yet there *was* something to be observed."' (p.294)

The relationship between these two characters, and the manner in which the dynamic between them and the Prefect of Police is central to the narrative, is discussed in the Story-by-Story section. What is important to note here is that, unlike the narrator of 'The Fall of the House of Usher', the narrator of the 'The Murders in the Rue Morgue' and 'The Purloined Letter' is clearly an individual with a distinct personality and his own views on matters.

This is best illustrated by a passage in 'The Purloined Letter', in which Dupin relates his views on the ability of those versed purely in the study of mathematics to reason well, and the narrator notes with dry humour: "You have a quarrel on hand, I see ... with some of the algebraists of Paris; but proceed" (p.444). The narrator is gently mocking his friend, who has become agitated over a matter that the narrator clearly does not think is quite as important as Dupin does.

Incidents such as these demonstrate the individuality of the narrator and his ability to see clearly the failings of his friend as well as his talents; this in turn means that we can rely on the veracity (truthfulness) of the narrator's account. Poe's detective stories are tales of ratiocination: that is, of instances of the process of reasoning and drawing sound conclusions even in situations that seem to defy reason and logic. A reliable narrator is important if an extraordinary character such as Dupin is to be believable and convincing, and enhances the overall impact of the story.

Male–female relationships

Poe's stories are notably lacking in female characters. Berenice, Madeline Usher and the wife of the narrator in 'The Black Cat' are the only women to have any significant interaction with the main characters of a story, and even then, none of them utters a single word. Their interaction, though important for those stories, is minor, and the female characters themselves are not well defined. This aspect of Poe's short stories is discussed further in the Themes, Ideas & Values section.

Egæus and Berenice

Key quote

'I shuddered in her presence, and grew pale at her approach; yet bitterly lamenting her fallen and desolate condition, I called to mind that she had loved me long, and, in an evil moment, I spoke to her of marriage.' (p.157)

Egæus is significant amongst Poe's characters, as it is through him that we come closest to understanding the notable lack of strong relationships between Poe's male and female characters. The story that Egæus narrates is unusual. Despite being named 'Berenice' and featuring a character of the same name, it is in fact almost entirely about Egæus. While Berenice acts as a source of motivation for Egæus' actions, she does not instigate any of the action in the story and we learn little about her.

Because Egæus can only deal in intellectual abstractions, his relationship with Berenice lacks the usual hallmarks of a relationship between two people who are engaged to be married. The extraordinary fact that Berenice does not engage in any dialogue with Egæus is crucial to our understanding that she exists solely as an idea in Egæus' world. Despite Berenice's presence, the central relationship is internal. This results from a combination of two factors. Firstly, Egæus can only relate to ideas and abstractions; and secondly, Egæus' physical female counterpart does not possess a strong enough personality for him to maintain an intimate and mutually satisfying relationship. In this respect, Egæus can be seen as emblematic of the general detachment that Poe's male characters exhibit, especially in their relationships with women.

THEMES, IDEAS & VALUES

At first glance it seems as if there are two distinct kinds of stories in this selection: detective stories and horror stories, with no strong connection between them. If we take 'The Fall of the House of Usher' and compare it to 'The Murders in the Rue Morgue', the differences appear significant. The former is set in an imaginary location at an undisclosed time, with an unreliable narrator relating events that we cannot be sure whether to believe or to assume have been imagined. 'The Murders in the Rue Morgue', on the other hand, concerns eminently believable – if slightly exaggerated – characters, set in a real time and place (critics agree the story is set contemporaneously, around 1840). It also depicts events – the solving of crimes using evidence and logic – that we can easily imagine might have occurred.

Nevertheless, despite these strong contrasts, the stories are connected thematically in complex and interesting ways. In relating the differences, we can also begin to see how the stories are interrelated, and explore a number of recurrent themes, ideas and values.

The divided self

One common link is the idea of the human mind, and the way it works. In particular, Poe examines extreme states of his characters' psychologies. These extremes can be categorised as the forms of behaviour that arise from the unconscious or irrational mind on the one hand, and the forms of behaviour that arise from the conscious, rational mind on the other. That is, some stories examine the ways in which fears, phobias and obsessions can cause people to do strange and terrible things, and to experience events that they scarcely believe are possible. Other stories examine the logical and rational operations of the human mind, through depicting characters who achieve remarkable outcomes of great benefit to themselves and others.

Irrationality and madness

Key quote

'At times, again, I was obliged to resolve all into the mere inexplicable vagaries of madness …' ('The Fall of the House of Usher', p.231)

The first category of behaviour is that controlled by the unconscious (or subconscious) mind. This side of the human psyche contains all those elements of human psychology that are innate, which do not come from rational thoughts and over which we have little or no control. These are things such as fears, phobias and obsessions. One critic has labelled this theme within Poe's short stories as 'the dissolution of personality' (Barinelli 1961, p.74).

As has been noted, most stories are narrated in the first person, which allows the reader unmediated access to the 'internal' perspective of characters, helping us to see events the way they do. This internal perspective is crucial in establishing and maintaining interest in the narrative. We are not simply witnessing abhorrent acts, such as premature burial, murder, cruelty to animals, deceit and adultery, which we tend to condemn automatically; we are viewing the world through the lens of madness and obsession. The stories examine irrational behaviour by representing the minds and beliefs of the protagonists. We see, for instance, what the world looks like from the point of view of someone who hears dead bodily organs, or sees their own double, or views bodily markings as omens, or believes the stones in the walls to be sentient (knowing and thinking).

Poe thus provides us – imaginatively – with insights into the nature and effects of irrationality, in ways that mark subtle distinctions between individual experiences. Some characters, for instance, exhibit irrational behaviour of which they are unaware, and for whom, it would seem, nothing can be done. Others, though, are aware of their obsessions and try to overcome them – successfully in the case of the narrator of 'The Premature Burial', but not in the case of Roderick Usher. Still others have a degree of self-awareness but give in to the darkness of the irrational part of their psyche, and must be judged accordingly.

One example of this distinction can be seen by comparing the narrators of 'The Tell-Tale Heart' and 'The Black Cat'. The narrator of the former, convinced of his own sanity, is effectively portrayed by the author as in the grip of a madness he is helpless to control. The narrator of 'The Black Cat', on the other hand, is aware that his rage and his 'dissolution' are controlling his actions. The irrational part of his mind dictates that he will harm his pets and his wife, and he knowingly gives in to it:

> from the sudden, frequent, and ungovernable outbursts of a fury to which I now blindly abandoned myself, my uncomplaining wife, alas! was the most usual and the most patient of sufferers. (p.397)

In between these two characters is the narrator of 'The Premature Burial', who does not at first realise that his irrational fear of being mistaken for dead is in fact causing his illness, although he later becomes aware of this. Thus, many characters in Poe's stories are prone to behaviour arising from the irrational part of the psyche, but they exhibit varying degrees of self-awareness and of self-control.

Another useful comparison is between Egæus and Roderick Usher. Roderick Usher is aware that his health is declining, and writes to the narrator about 'a mental disorder which oppressed him … with a view of attempting … some alleviation of his malady' (p.217). Roderick is aware of his illness and his irrational tendencies, and he also seeks to cure himself. In light of this, his capitulation to a state of insanity at the end of the story evokes sadness and dismay in the reader.

In contrast, Egæus seems perfectly accepting of a condition whose symptoms, notably a 'nervous *intensity of interest*' (p.155), result in obsessive trance-like states. Egæus does not appear to have the slightest interest in lifting himself out of this condition, and indeed seems resigned to his fate. This element of the story is compounded when Egæus tells us that 'in an evil moment, I spoke to [Berenice] of marriage' (p.157). This is a highly ambiguous statement. Like the rest of the story, it is in the past tense, and may indicate that Egæus, looking back while telling his story, realises that no good could ever have come from someone in his condition marrying the ill Berenice. However, it could also be a tacit admission that at the time he thought of marriage, he knew it would result in harm to Berenice. In the final accounting, though his cousin is entombed alive in much the same manner as Madeline Usher, Egæus is a far more sinister character than Roderick Usher. He is less deserving of our empathy, as he has no desire to help himself, and may even be aware of the effect his irrational tendencies will inevitably have on others.

The manner in which Poe presents the irrationality of his characters is partly due to the effect he wished to achieve. Clearly in the case of Roderick Usher, Poe wants the reader to experience, among other things, a sense of pathos – or of compassion and pity – even if this is tinged with fear and horror. In the case of Egæus, however, these latter two emotions are the predominant ones that Poe seeks to arouse in the reader.

Rationality and reason

Key quote

'I dismissed forever my charnal apprehensions, and with them vanished the cataleptic disorder, of which, perhaps, they had been less the consequence than the cause.' ('The Premature Burial', p.429)

The second category of behaviour is an equal and exact opposite of the first (discussed above), and it is explored in stories examining the rational and reasoning part of our minds. C. August Dupin contrasts strongly with the characters who exhibit the irrational behaviours discussed above. The construction of Dupin's character is based almost entirely on reasoned answers and explanations; logic is central to the portrayal of his character, and therefore to what he represents. He does not allow predispositions to certain fears, phobias or irrational impulses to affect his thinking or lead him to unsound conclusions. Dupin embodies the idea that the conscious part of our minds can think rationally in all circumstances and solve any problem, no matter how mysterious or insoluble it appears.

Key point

In this way we see that the detective narratives simply represent the opposite side of the human mind to the narratives of the Gothic horror stories. In the Gothic horror stories we think we can explain events, but, as in 'The Black Cat', we can never be sure. In contrast, for Dupin, nothing, no matter how unusual, is without explanation.

Another character who uses his rational and intellectual abilities, and by doing so avoids a seemingly imminent death, is the prisoner in 'The Pit and the Pendulum'. The prisoner is able to free himself when he turns his concentration away from dwelling abstractly on the swinging pendulum, and instead focuses his mind on the concrete problem of his restraints. Like the Dupin stories with their attempt at a degree of historical verisimilitude (truthfulness) – but unlike 'The Masque of the Red Death' with its fantastic setting – the historical basis of the prisoner's circumstances makes it easier for the reader to find the prisoner's thoughts and behaviour to be plausible and believable. Because the setting is less open to doubt, the events of the story, as described by the prisoner, are placed much more firmly in the reader's mind as a rational account of specific and realistic (although terrifying) events.

Entrapment

Key quote

'I felt nothing; yet dreaded to move a step, lest I should be impeded by the walls of a *tomb*.' ('The Pit and the Pendulum', p.370)

Entrapment has a variety of causes in these stories, but invariably has a similar effect. For Poe, entrapment symbolises the detachment and isolation of characters from the world around them. Characters can suffer from entrapment within a house, an inquisitor's prison, a tomb, or even within the metaphorical prison created by their own fears, as in the case of the narrator of 'The Premature Burial'. In each case they are detached from healthy activity and from contact with other people. Whether their entrapment is of their own making or not, the detachment it fosters leads to suffering in one form or another for the characters so affected.

The theme of entrapment is particularly noticeable as Poe often uses striking visual imagery to present it. In particular, Poe's architectural symbolism is a powerful element that highlights the manner in which characters are trapped by their circumstances, and sometimes by their own life choices.

The use of Gothic symbolism to illustrate entrapment is evident, for example, when the narrator of 'The Cask of Amontillado' leads Fortunato 'through several suites of rooms ... down a long and winding staircase ... [to] the damp ground of the catacombs of the Montresors' (p.498). The house is important in evoking an atmosphere: catacombs are, after all, subterranean burial chambers. Fortunato is thus doubly entrapped, when Montresor entombs him within what was once a tomb.

In the case of 'The Cask of Amontillado', Poe utilises entrapment as the culmination of the story; however, it is a more permanent feature of the lives of characters in other stories. Again, architecture can be seen as representative of circumstances that help to define characters. Secluded Gothic mansions in 'Berenice' and 'William Wilson' convey the idea of an extravagant, yet isolated and detached upbringing. Both protagonists have been shaped by the entrapment of their childhoods. However, whereas Egæus remains trapped in the structures of his youth, unable to escape their confines and live a meaningful life outside of the influence of the 'Gothic', Wilson was compelled to leave the large and mysterious building in which he boarded at Dr. Bransby's school. Wilson recalls the building as a 'quaint old building ... veritably a palace of enchantment' (p.241). The architectural symbolism in this story is mixed: although Wilson looks back with fondness on the school building, it was also clearly a dark and labyrinthine place, as much a prison for the boarders as their school.

Architecture, and through it the circumstance of physical entrapment, is also used by Poe to convey ideas that relate to the story as a whole, and not merely to the characters. An example is 'The Masque of the Red Death', in which events take place in 'the deep seclusion of one of [Prospero's] castellated abbeys. This was an extensive and magnificent structure' (p.359). In this tale, however, the fortress becomes a prison. As in 'The Cask of Amontillado', the imprisonment of Prince Prospero and his guests is important for the creation of tension in the story – when we realise that the revellers are trapped with Death in their midst – and also for the creation of a sense of punishment, emphasising the story's role as a moral tale.

Entrapment is not always a condition that befalls characters by chance, and it is important to consider the degree to which the characters' entrapment is of their own making. The narrator of 'The Premature Burial' has a cataleptic affliction that makes him afraid 'that, upon awaking, I might find myself the tenant of a grave' (p.423). In a twist, this fear of being 'nailed up in some common coffin—and thrust, deep, deep, and forever, into some ordinary and nameless *grave*' (p.428), has led the narrator to become a virtual prisoner. As he observes, 'I hesitated to ride, or to walk, or to indulge in any exercise that would carry me from home' (p.425). The narrator's fear of entombment has led him to become entrapped, afraid to stray too far from home or to mingle with those he does not know.

Entombment is an obvious symbol for the entrapment of the individual, and is used to good effect in 'The Fall of the House of Usher'. When the narrator of this story meets Roderick Usher, he observes that: 'In the manner of my friend I was at once struck with an incoherence ... an excessive nervous agitation' (p.221). However, Roderick Usher's mental health declines even more markedly after the entombment of his sister:

> And now, some days of bitter grief having elapsed, an observable change came over the features of the mental disorder of my friend ... The pallor of his countenance had assumed, if possible, a more ghastly hue—but the luminousness of his eye had utterly gone out. (p.231)

As in 'The Premature Burial', a double layer of entrapment can be seen. Roderick Usher was already trapped within his house, apparently afraid or unable to leave. As in the case of Egæus and the narrator of 'The Premature Burial', this seclusion has caused him to become physically and mentally unwell. But when he buries his sister – who, like Roderick, represents the last of the line of Ushers, and whose burial therefore symbolises the end of that lineage – he entombs her in a temporary mausoleum that is effectively a prison of his own making. The layers of entrapment reflect Roderick's gradual retreat from the outside world, and from the normality of regular exercise, travel and social contact, a life in which one does not dwell on thoughts of death, as the narrator of 'The Premature Burial' tells us (p.429). By entrapping his sister in this manner, Roderick condemns the House of Usher to oblivion.

Illness and death

Key quotes

'Hitherto she had steadily borne up against the pressure of her malady, and had not betaken herself finally to bed; but on the closing in of the evening of my arrival at the house, she succumbed …' ('The Fall of the House of Usher', p.224)

'No pestilence had ever been so fatal, or so hideous. Blood was its Avator and its seal—the redness and the horror of blood.' ('The Masque of the Red Death', p.359)

Illness and death were expected in tales of Gothic horror, and Poe provided them. However, Poe's tales represent an evolution of the genre, and we can see in these stories that the *supernatural* as an explanation for the plight of characters has been replaced with the *psychological*. Illness, death and madness are inextricably linked in the stories of Poe. In many instances, though, it is the case that disease, and the prospect or event of death, are used by Poe to explore the irrational aspects of the human psyche.

Poe makes extensive use of visual symbolism to represent illness and death. The two are often presented together, as was common in the Gothic genre, and this is especially so in 'The Masque of the Red Death'. Illness equates to suffering and inevitable death, as we see when the symptoms and progression of the plague are described: 'the whole seizure, progress and termination of the disease, were the incidents of half an hour' (p.359).

The representation of illness in the Gothic is inextricably connected to death through the motif (idea or image) of decay. The incarnation of 'Red Death', which stalks the halls of Prince Prospero's party, is symbolic not only of death, but also of 'Darkness and Decay' which 'held illimitable dominion over all' (p.366). Similarly, in 'The Cask of Amontillado', Montresor guides Fortunato through 'the damp ground' (p.498) of catacombs whose 'walls had been lined with human remains, piled to the vault overhead' (p.500). The desired effect is clear: as the unwitting Fortunato coughs his way drunkenly through the catacombs, the pervasive architectural symbolism of death, reinforced by Fortunato's illness (his cough) and the general sense of decay – suggested by the dampness, the 'foulness of the air' (p.500) and the human remains – make the outcome appear inevitable. It is this terrible inevitability that generates the chilling effect of the story.

Architectural symbolism also conveys the notion of death and decay in 'The Fall of the House of Usher'. The house is in a state of 'extraordinary dilapidation' and 'extensive decay' (p.219); it also has the appearance of a skull with 'vacant eye-like windows' (p.216), symbolising its connection not only to the ailing line of Ushers, but also to death.

Inherited illness

The idea of inherited diseases which are vague in nature but debilitating in effect, and which result in bizarre or monstrous behaviour, is a common one in Gothic fiction, and had become a stereotype even in Poe's day. As with the architectural symbolism on which Poe relied so heavily, however, it is clear he found the continued fascination this theme held for readers to be irresistible.

In 'The Fall of the House of Usher', for instance, the obvious visual symbols of death overlay a more complex representation of illness. Roderick's malady is a 'constitutional and a family evil' (p.222). Roderick suffers both physically, from illness, which the author confirms when he tells us that Roderick has a 'cadaverousness of complexion' (p.221), and mentally from the irrational fear he experiences. There is a blurring of the boundary here between illness and madness. We see this also in the case of William Wilson. Wilson's parents are 'beset with constitutional infirmities', the result of an 'inherited family character', of which Wilson himself is a victim, and which has resulted in his 'evil propensities' (p.239).

The case of the narrator of 'The Premature Burial' is instructive. His fears have led to his 'disease' of catalepsy, for which the 'cure' is a healthier, more active lifestyle, with less reading of horror stories. In fact, Poe's descriptions of incidences of cataleptic illness are so extravagantly heavy-handed, that it is clear he does not give much credence to the idea of such a disease, a reading which is reinforced by the conclusion. The narrator's disease is secondary to his irrational fear, and for Poe, the presence of illness is not as significant as the presence of mental disorders such as obsession and paranoia. This is also the case with Fortunato's illness, a cough which is exacerbated by the nitre in Montresor's catacombs. The fact that Fortunato is ill simply does not possess the significance of Montresor's delusional compulsion to take revenge, even though its place in the narrative is important in the creation of dramatic effect.

The absence of values

Identifying the values possessed or demonstrated by Poe's characters can be problematic. Many of the stories are concerned with the psychology of the characters – with what is going on in their minds. This does not make for a great deal of interaction between characters, and when it does, such interaction is often malevolent in nature. In seeking to identify values in literature, we are generally looking for evidence in the behaviour of characters that indicates that they hold certain values ahead of others. This immediately causes a problem, for the characters in these stories often exhibit behaviour which is undesirable and at times immoral.

The stories do not present us immediately and obviously with positive values and ideals. Instead, it is necessary to look beneath the surface to find them. A simple way of doing this is to observe that the characters' attitudes and beliefs often represent the opposite of the values the author is actually endorsing.

Conscience

Key quote

> 'But anything was better than this agony! Anything was more tolerable than this derision! I could bear those hypocritical smiles no longer! I felt that I must scream or die! ... "Villains!" I shrieked, "dissemble no more! I admit the deed! ..."' ('The Tell-Tale Heart', p.389)

One of the main actions undertaken by the characters is to cause harm or suffering to others as a result of their own fears, uncertainties or madness. Through these actions, Poe examines the consequences of living in a world where conscience has little or no power, a world in which there are no moral consequences for the perpetrators of violence or other crimes.

The exploration of this value is complicated by the fact that, largely due to the use of first-person narration, we are inclined to sympathise with the protagonist until we discover just where their delusions have led them. In 'Berenice', for example, we have no particular reason to condemn Egæus until we learn that he has desecrated his cousin's tomb and body. That these actions were carried out while in a trance he could not control, because of an obsession he does not fully understand, is symbolic of his inability to conscientiously consider the consequences and morality of his actions.

Similarly, Roderick Usher, who is the slave of his own terror, buries his sister alive. Montresor does the same to Fortunato in 'The Cask of Amontillado', for reasons that he does not clearly elaborate and which it is impossible for us to judge the validity of. The blind obsession of these characters is closely tied to their lack of conscience, a trait that might have prevented them from undertaking these torments.

Poe often uses characters who appear helpless to prevent themselves from engaging in acts of cruelty. The narrator of 'The Tell-Tale Heart' has an obsession with the Old Man's eye that he cannot explain or rationalise to us, while the narrator of 'The Black Cat' appears helpless to control his anger towards himself and others. Both characters cause others to suffer – to die, in fact – as a result of their own inner demons and anguish. This creates a drama, and draws the reader into the story by showing us the world of the criminal. The challenge is to look beyond these characters' descriptions of events that centre on their own suffering, and to realise that their actions can only take place in the absence of conscience. Poe contrasts the viewpoints of these characters with the viewpoints of those such as the prisoner of 'The Pit and the Pendulum', whose suffering can only result from the lack of conscience on the part of his tormenters.

Ultimately, these stories suggest that conscience is the psychological mechanism by which individuals restrain themselves from inflicting harm on others. The characters do not have the right to do many of the things that they do, but the fact that an action is criminal or immoral is not enough to prevent its occurrence in these stories. Depicting not simply these actions but the states of mind that lead to them, Poe illustrates the value of conscience – by showing the effects of its absence. The stories thus warn us of the consequences of lives lived without conscience.

Weakness in women

Key quote

'... in the silence of my library at night, she had flitted by my eyes, and I had seen her—not as the living and breathing Berenice, but as the Berenice of a dream—not as a being of the earth, earthy, but as the abstraction of such a being—not as a thing to admire, but to analyze—not as an object of love, but as the theme of the most abstruse although desultory speculation.' ('Berenice', p.157)

The general lack of female characters, and the relatively trivial role and weak nature of those female characters present, does not reflect well on Poe in the twenty-first century. Women in Poe's stories, consistent with texts from the Gothic genre up until that time, were generally beautiful and mysterious, and invariably suffered before dying tragically at a young age. The characters Berenice and Madeline Usher conform almost exactly to this inherited stereotype. The stories generally place little or no value on women, let alone on ideals such as gender equality.

Of course, Poe's stories must be read within the context of his time, although this does not excuse the attitudes they embody. Poe himself attended university in Virginia, where he studied French and Classics. His stories reflect his high level of education in the liberal arts: they are peppered with untranslated quotes from classic texts in foreign languages. The clear evidence of his level of education indicates that his writing was targeted for others who were similarly well educated. This necessarily meant he was writing for a predominantly male audience, as women did not generally attend university in the first half of the nineteenth century. Indeed some universities, such as the University of Oxford in England, did not admit women until well into the twentieth century, almost one hundred years after the time Poe was writing. From this perspective then, the lack of strong female characters results from a mix of the prejudices of the day, and the commercial need to write stories that would appeal to a predominantly conservative male readership.

Critics agree, however, that a key reason for the continual appearance of weak female characters is the difficult and often traumatic relationships that Poe had with women (see the Background & Context section for more on these biographical details). Perhaps the most telling lines from these stories are those in the 'key quote' above. If we read these lines as being at least partly an expression of Poe's own views, and not simply as representing Egæus' view of Berenice, they assist readers to contextualise the value, or rather, the lack of value, placed on women in these stories. We can read the representations of women in these stories as a reflection of Poe's inability to engage with the women in his life, perhaps because of the sadness with which his relationships with women often seemed to end. This manifests itself in the texts as the reduction of women to objects of beauty and sadness, with whom no meaningful or lasting engagement is possible.

DIFFERENT INTERPRETATIONS

Different interpretations arise from different responses to a text. There is no single correct reading or interpretation of a text. However, an interpretation is more than an 'opinion' – it is the justification of a point of view on the text as a whole or on one element of it. To present an interpretation of the text based on your point of view, you must use a logical argument and relevant evidence from the text to support and strengthen it.

The following paragraphs outline two possible interpretations of the stories' overall meaning and significance.

A pessimistic view of humanity

This interpretation sees the stories as reflecting Poe's profoundly pessimistic view of humanity. The stories show humanity at its lowest ebb, and are linked by the common darkness of the circumstances in which they take place. The stories together present the view that people cannot help but hurt themselves and others. They suggest that madness is unavoidable, and is indeed welcomed by many. They reinforce the idea that not only is death inevitable, but murder is a common occurrence.

The characters are a strange assortment of the mad and the obsessed, the violent and the murderous. The narrator of 'The Tell-Tale Heart' is a prime example of Poe's bleak view of humanity. At the outset of the story, he confesses that for no reason other than his desire to 'rid' himself of an old man's eye 'forever', he 'made up [his] mind to take the life of the old man' (p.384). Furthermore, the narrator remains unmoved by the experience of his gruesome actions, as he admits when he says: 'calmly I can tell you the whole story' (p.384).

Even colder than this, are the actions of Montresor in 'The Cask of Amontillado', who is convinced of the 'thousand injuries of Fortunato' (p.496). Montresor does not say what these injuries are, although his ability to lift heavy bricks in order to make a wall indicates that Fortunato has not done him physical harm. Nonetheless, although the narrator hears the condemned man scream to him, *'For the love of God, Montresor!'* (p.503), he is implacable, and continues to seal Fortunato up alive in a tomb.

Another of Poe's characters who kills without reason is the narrator of 'The Black Cat', who does so in the full knowledge that his actions are both illegal and morally reprehensible. Of his 'favourite pet' Pluto, he tells us that: 'One morning in cool blood, I slipped a noose about its neck and hung it to the limb of a tree' (p.393). However, this is not enough for the narrator who, 'goaded, by the interference' of his wife, 'buried [an] axe in her brain' (p.398).

Madness plagues the characters of Poe's stories, and drives them to extreme actions. In 'Berenice', Egæus confesses that he has been afflicted with monomania, and that, even worse, his beautiful cousin Berenice suffers from 'a fatal disease', which 'fell like the simoom (hot desert wind) upon her frame' (p.154). Despite her suffering, or perhaps because of it, he admits that 'my disorder revelled in the less important but more startling changes wrought in the *physical* frame of Berenice—in the singular and most appalling distortion of her personal identity' (p.157). As if this is not enough, Egæus then exhumes the body of the (seemingly) recently deceased Berenice and removes her teeth.

Madness and death seem inextricably linked in the mind of the author, who combines the two in 'The Fall of the House of Usher'. The narrator informs us that his friend Roderick Usher is 'a bounden slave' to terror (p.222). This madness leads Roderick to prematurely entomb his sister and prevents him from coming to Madeline's aid – which leads in turn to her actual death. On the night of a wild storm, when the house of Usher is collapsing and something sinister approaches on the stairs, Roderick tells the narrator that for 'many minutes, many hours, many days' (p.236) he has heard the sounds of his sister trying to escape her tomb, and yet has done nothing to assist her.

Characters are the instruments of the author, and through their actions we can see an expression of Poe's views of the inherent nature of humanity. The behaviour of the central characters in these stories is marked by numerous criminal acts and experiences of madness, revealing Poe's view of humanity to be a profoundly pessimistic one.

Divine justice operates in the world

This more positive interpretation sees the stories as presenting a world view in which those guilty of crimes will be punished and divine justice operates. The stories contain many examples of foul deeds, as well as instances of insanity and obsession; however, in all these cases the guilty receive some form of punishment for their transgressions. In some instances the punishment does not derive from any clear source, but those who harm others nonetheless suffer for their crimes. Indeed, in some instances those guilty of crimes are compelled by some inner force to make sure they are punished. Taken together, the stories promote the author's essentially optimistic view that, although there is evil in the world and in the hearts of some people, there is also a kind of divine justice that seeks to redress the wrongs done by humanity.

One character who commits a villainous act, and then subconsciously ensures that he is caught and punished, is the narrator of 'The Tell-Tale Heart'. Although he has murdered the old man and hidden his dismembered body under the floorboards, he is nonetheless compelled to give himself away. The narrator believes he can hear the beating of the dead man's 'hideous heart', a noise that grows 'louder—louder—*louder!*'(p.389). But this is patently ridiculous, as a dead heart cannot beat, and there is no sound to disturb the policemen who 'chatted pleasantly and smiled' (p.389). Earlier the narrator declares his belief that he can hear 'all the things in the heaven and the earth' (p.384). Clearly, however, the maddening beating is in fact the sound of his own guilty heart, compelling him to confess to his terrible crime.

Confessing one's crimes is an idea we also find in the story 'The Cask of Amontillado', although it is less obvious. Montresor, feeling that he suffered a 'thousand' injuries at the hands of Fortunato, exacted revenge, and sealed Fortunato up alive in the catacombs below his house. But even in the face of such a cold-blooded crime, the guilty conscience gnaws away at the murderer. Montresor acknowledges at the end of the tale that 'For the half of a century no mortal has disturbed' the tomb of Fortunato (p.503). From this we can tell that Montresor is relating his tale to us fifty years after his crime, when he is no doubt an old man. What would compel him to do such a thing? He is of course confessing to his crime, and he alludes to the suffering he has undergone as a result of it, as he relates the tale to 'You, who so well know the nature of my soul' (p.496).

'William Wilson' suggests that the conscience of humanity is strong, even in the face of a great desire to ignore it. Wilson acknowledges that he has 'evil propensities' (p.239), and spends his life engaged in 'miserable profligacy' (p.251). However, Wilson's double, whom we understand to be the physical incarnation of Wilson's conscience, pursues him though Europe, from the site of one misdeed to another. Wilson is desperate to escape this mysterious version of himself: 'From his inscrutable tyranny did I at length flee, panic-stricken' (p.258). Later, though, he realises that he '*fled in vain*' (p.258). Finally, he is forced to face his double – at which point he tries to kill his conscience in order to banish all thoughts of guilt. But as his double dies, it also pronounces the death of Wilson's own identity, highlighting the futility of trying to remove one's feelings of guilt or sense of morality.

Perhaps the clearest indication that individuals cannot escape reckoning for their actions comes in 'The Masque of the Red Death'. In this tale a powerful individual, Prince Prospero, seeks to hide himself from a world full of death and suffering. While others die he is heedless, choosing to retreat into a 'castellated abbey' which is then sealed, in order that 'the courtiers might bid defiance to contagion' and the outside world can 'take care of itself' (p.360). However, even a man of power and influence such as Prince Prospero is accountable for his actions in the eyes of the author. And so Death himself, 'masqued' with the plague of the Red Death, enters the abbey and 'one by one dropped the revellers in the blood-bedewed halls of their revel' (p.366).

The fates that befall these characters indicate the author's optimistic view that no matter the circumstances of an individual's transgressions, ultimately there is no escaping retribution for evil deeds.

QUESTIONS & ANSWERS

The essay topics below show a range of possible styles and formats, and are suitable for senior English assessment tasks and examinations.

Essay topics

1. 'The characters in Poe's stories are essentially similar and exhibit few differences.' Discuss.
2. 'These stories are simply scary tales, with no deeper meaning.' Do you agree?
3. How does Poe explore the effects of fear on human behaviour?
4. 'The stories convey nothing more than the author's obsession with death and dying.' Is this your view of the stories?
5. 'Poe is primarily concerned with the inherent weakness of people when they are under pressure.' Discuss.
6. 'The use of first-person narration in the stories leads us to sympathise with the characters.' Discuss.
7. 'The stories suggest that relationships are of little importance in life.' Discuss.
8. 'The extreme and unusual settings and contexts of the stories mean their events can be dismissed as having no real significance.' Discuss.
9. 'The honesty of Poe's characters means we can accept their accounts as entirely truthful.' Discuss.
10. Why do Poe's characters struggle to impose order on their worlds?

Analysing a sample topic

'The stories suggest that relationships are of little importance in life.' Discuss.

Firstly, take the time to clearly understand the question. It helps to highlight the key words and phrases. This question is made up of two parts. Firstly, the contention that the stories suggest relationships are of little importance. Secondly, the basis for the contention: that there are few relationships and these are not well developed. The key phrases are 'few relationships' and 'of little importance in life'.

Consider your own position and formulate a contention. It is not necessary to simply agree. Questions often invite an opposing viewpoint through the use of broad statements.

Collect the material needed to support your position. This includes making notes about the passages you may refer to, as well as quotes you intend to use. The evidence you use may include passages and quotes that:

- support the contention by showing that there are few relationships and that characters find other aspects of their lives to be more important; or
- dispute the contention by showing relationships in the text that have great importance for the characters; or
- dispute the contention by showing the suffering of characters with few or no relationships, demonstrating by contrast the importance placed on relationships by the stories.

Write your response so that it is *consistent* and *clearly structured*. All essays should consist of an introduction, a body and a conclusion.

The **introduction** should outline the argument being made. A strong opening paragraph with a definite position on the given contention will grab the attention of the reader and let them know what you are going to be saying.

The **body** will consist of several paragraphs that move through the evidence from the text in support of your overall argument. Try not to fit too much into one paragraph: a paragraph should present one main idea. To produce a coherent answer, ensure the paragraphs are logically connected. In particular, use one or more linking words to make a connection between the last sentence of a paragraph and the first sentence of the next paragraph.

The **conclusion** should draw together the points made in the body of the essay, to support and conclusively demonstrate the main argument (which was presented in the introduction). Avoid too much repetition of the introduction; don't simply restate verbatim what you have already written.

SAMPLE ANSWER

'The honesty of Poe's characters means we can accept their accounts as entirely truthful.' Discuss.

The characters in these stories by Edgar Allan Poe are presented in a wide variety of settings, with significant variation in their personal circumstances. Some of the characters, such as C. Auguste Dupin, are in a setting that is relatively realistic – that of nineteenth-century Paris – and display behaviour that, while remarkable, is not significantly abnormal. However, other characters are in highly unusual situations, and display behaviour that calls into question the reliability of their testimony. These characters can be relied upon to be objective in their relation of events only insofar as they *believe* they are giving a truthful account. This behaviour is demonstrated in particular by characters such as Roderick Usher and William Wilson, whose account of events can often be called into question.

Roderick Usher is clearly a man whose sanity is on the verge of collapse. The narrator finds Roderick to be a 'hypochondriac' and subject to a 'habitual trepidancy—an excessive nervous agitation'. Roderick is beset by fear, and is also depressed at the thought that his sister, Madeline, might soon die of a strange illness. These trying personal circumstances suggest that Roderick's sanity and grasp of reality might be diminished. This is confirmed when the narrator relates that Roderick has 'superstitious impressions in regard to the dwelling which he tenanted' – that is, Roderick believes that the building he inhabits is sentient and has a life of its own. Roderick's tenuous grip on reality must therefore lead us to doubt the accuracy of his pronouncement that his sister has died. When Roderick makes it clear to the narrator that he distrusts Madeline's doctors, we realise that the doctors have not had a chance to examine her body for themselves in order to confirm her demise. In this way we can see the problems inherent in Roderick's version of events: while Roderick may believe Madeline to have died, we cannot be sure that what Roderick has perceived is really the case.

A similar discrepancy occurs during William Wilson's relation of events after he has 'effected' the 'total ruin' of Glendinning by cheating at cards. We understand from the final scene of the story, when Wilson has stabbed his double but sees himself bleeding in the mirror, that the double that pursues him is his own conscience. The fantastic nature of this knowledge calls into question Wilson's assertions about the scene with Glendinning. Wilson relates that the doors were thrown open 'as if by magic', and 'every candle in the room' was 'extinguished'. The room is cast into darkness, and the occupants 'could only *feel* that he [the stranger] was standing in our midst'. Thus no-one actually sees the intruder, whose voice, Wilson tells us, is – conveniently – a whispered version of his own. The strange intruder departs before the candles can be re-lit. We realise that although he denies feeling guilty, Wilson is literally plagued by his own guilt. We must therefore question whether there was 'a stranger' at all, and whether Wilson did not in fact give himself away as a cheat.

These examples illustrate that Poe's characters invariably describe events that they believe to be true. However, by carefully examining their version of events, and taking into account the circumstances in which they find themselves, we can sometimes question the veracity of their claims. Poe's characters cannot always be relied upon to objectively recount the true nature of events that occur around them and in which they are involved. The 'truth' they relate is thus a subjective one, as it is often a true account only of what characters believe to have taken place.

REFERENCES & READING

Text

Poe, EA 2004, *Great Short Works of Edgar Allan Poe*, ed. GR Thompson, Perennial Classics, New York.

Criticism and background

Buranelli, V 1961, *Edgar Allan Poe*, Twaynes Publishers Inc., New York.

Television

Edgar Allan Poe: Terror of the Soul 1995, dir. Joyce Chopra & Karen Thomas, Film Odyssey Inc.

Documentary on Poe's life and work, including an adaptation of 'The Cask of Amontillado'.

'The Raven' in *Treehouse of Horror (The Simpsons Halloween Special)*, first broadcast 25 October 1990 (Season 2, Episode 3), dir. Wesley Archer, Rich Moore & David Silverman, Gracie Films.
This episode available on the DVD The Best of The Simpsons. Vol. 4, *20th Century Fox.*

Website

The Edgar Allan Poe Society of Baltimore, www.eapoe.org